Great Mozart Arias
for Soprano

Voice and Piano

WOLFGANG AMADEUS
MOZART

DOVER PUBLICATIONS, INC.
Mineola, New York

NOTE

With Mozart, opera at last came fully alive, and the characters on stage began to have definite musical personality. As a result, Mozart not only seems to speak the same operatic language as we do—to give us what we expect from opera— but has virtually invalidated everything that went before. He was the first to perceive clearly the vast possibilities of the form as a means of creating characters, great and small, who moved, thought, and breathed musically like human beings. His singers discarded the masks of Greek drama, as it were, and appeared as individuals with a recognizable personality; they took an active part instead of looking and commenting.

It is hardly surprising that Mozart should have taken instinctively to the form of Italian opera: his musical upbringing was wholly Italian and his temperament was characteristic of that eighteenth-century cosmopolitanism that made Italian the *lingua franca* of cultured musical society. That *Die Entführung aus dem Serail* and *Die Zauberflöte* should both have been composed to German texts is of no great relevance; for while it was through Italian opera that Mozart came to express and develop his genius for the theater and for the creation of human musical characters, in the end it is the music by which he achieves his ends that matters—music which in its depth and variety, its color and wit, gives its composer a universality and peculiar sublimity unique in the whole history of music.

Adapted from Spike Hughes'
A Listener's Guide to Mozart's Great Operas
(Dover Publications, 1972: 0-486-22858-4)

CONTENTS

Great Mozart Arias
for Soprano

Idomeneo, rè di Creta

Idomeneo, King of Crete
κ366 (1781)

[1] QUANDO AVRAN FINE OMAI—PADRE, GERMANI, ADDIO!

Recitative

Andantino

Quando avran fi_ne o_ma_i l'a_spre sventu_re mi_e?

Ilia in_fe_li_ce! Di tem_pe_sta cru_del mi_se_ro a_

van_zo, del ge_ni_tor, e de' ger_ma_ni pri_va del bar_ba_ro ne_

mi_co mi_sto col sangue il san_gue vit_ti_me ge_ne_ro_se a qual

Allegro

sor_te più re_a ti ri_ser_ba_no i Nu_mi?

Pur ven_di_ca_ste vo_i, di Pri_a_mo e di Troja i danni e l'onte?

Pe_ri la flot ta Ar_gi_va, e Idome_ne_o pa_sto for_se sa_ra d'or_ca vo_

ra_ce... ma che mi giova, o ciel! se al primo aspetto di quel

pro_de I_da_man_te, che all'on_de mi ra_pì, l'o_dio de_po_si, e

Andante agitato

Adagio

tor, o prence, o sorte! o vi_ta sventu_ra_ta, o dol _ ce

morte! Ma che? m'ama I_da_mante?

Allegro

Ah no; l'ingrato per E_let_tra sos_pi_ra, e quell'E_lettra meschi_na princi_

pes _ sa, e _ su_le d'Ar_go, d'O _ res_te al_le scia_gu_re a que_ste a_

re_ne fug_gi_ti_va, ra_min_ga, è mia ri_va_le.

Aria

Andante con moto

co-re.   Padre, ger-ma-ni, ad-di-o! voi

fo-ste,   io vi per-de-i,   voi fo-ste,   io vi per-de-i.

Gre - cia, ca-gion tu se-i,   Gre - cia, ca-gion tu

se-i,   e un gre-co a-do-re-rò?   e un gre-co a-do-re-

rò?   un gre_co   a _ do _ re _ rò?   D'in_

gra_ta al san_gue mi _ o   sò, che la col_pa a_vre_i;   ma quel sem_

bian_te, oh De_i! o _ dia _ _ re an _ cor __ non sò.   D'in_

gra_ta al sangue mi_o   sò, che la col_pa a_rrei;   ma quel sem_

Allegro assai

sento, fu _ rie del cru _ do a _ ver _ _ no,

fu _ rie del cru _ do a _ ver _ no, lunge a si gran tor _

mento a _ mor, mer _ cè, pie _ tù, a _ mor, mer _ cè, pie _

tù. Chi mi rubò quel co _ re,

quel che tra _ di _ to ha il mi _ o, quel che tra _

det _ tae cru _ del _ tà, ven_det _ tae cru _ del _ tà, ven_

det _ tae cru _ del _ tà, ven _ _det _ tae cru _ del_

tà, e cru _ _ del _ tà.

Tut _ te nel cor vi

sen_to, vi sen_to, vi sen_to, fu _ rie del cru_doa _

ver _ _ no,   fu _ rie del cru _ doa _ ver _ _

no,   del cru _ doa _ ver _ _ no,   lunge a si gran tor _ mento   a _

mor,   mercè, pie _ tà,   a _ mor   mer _ cè,   pie _ tà!

Chi mi ru _ bò   quel co _ re,

quel che tra_di _ to hail mi _ o,   quel   che   tra_di _ to,   tra_

det _ ta e cru _ del_tà,   ven_det_ta e cru _ del_tà,   ven _ det _ ta e
cru _ del _ tà,   ven _ det _ ta e   cru _ del _ _ tà, ven_det ta e
cru _ del _ tà, vendetta e cru _ _ del _ _ tà.

Andante, ma sostenuto

mezza voce

padre per_de_i, la patria il ri_po_so, tu pa_dre mi se_i,

tu pa_dre mi se_i, tu

pa _ dre mi se _ i,   sog _ giorno amoroso

è Creta__ per me.   Or più   non rammen _ to   l'an_

go _ scie,   gli af_fanni, gli af _ fan _ _ ni,   or gioja e con_

ten_to, compenso a miei dan _ ni il cie_lo mi diè,   compenso a miei

danni il cie - lo mi diè, or gio _ _ _ ja e con_

ten _ _ _ _ _ to il cie _ _ lo __ mi diè.

Se il padre per_de_i, la

patria, il ri _ po_so, tu pa_dre__ mi se _ i, tu,

_to il cie_lo mi diè,   il cie _ lo mi diè,   il cie _ lo mi

diè.

[4] IDOL MIO, SE RITROSO ALTRO AMANTE
—ODO DA LUNGE ARMONIOSO SUONO

ste _ ro amor.   Scaccie _ ra _   vi _ ci _ no ar_

dore   dal tuo sen l'ar_dor lon _ta _ no, l'ardor lon _ tano;

più la ma _ no può d'a _ mo _ re s'è vi _ cin l'a _ mante cor,

l'a _   _ man _ te cor,   più la ma _ no

può d'a _ mo _ re sè vi _ cin l'a mante cor, l'a _ man _ _ _ _ _ _ _ te

cor, l'a _ man _ te cor, l'a _ man _ te cor.

I _ dol mi_o, se ri _ troso altro a_mante a me ti ren _ de, non m'of_

staccato

cin la_mante cor, l'a _ _ man _ te cor,

piu la ma_no può d'a_mo_re s'è vi_cin l'aman_te

cor, l'a _ _man _ _ _ _ _

_ _ _ te cor, s'è vicin l'amante cor, s'è vi_

cin l'a_mante cor, l'a_man _ te cor, l'a_man _ te

Marcia

cor.

p assai

pp

O _ do da lun _ ge ar _ mo _ ni _ o _ so suo _ no, che mi chiama all'im _

bar _ co, or _ sù si va _ da.

tr

do_ro, che mi ser_ bi il cor__ fe_del.   Zef_fi_ret_ ti lu_sin_

ghie_ri, deh vola_ te al mio te_so_ro, e gli dite, chio l'a_ doro,

che mi serbi il cor__ fe_del, che mi ser_ bi il cor__ fe_

del,_____ il cor___ fe_del,_____

_____ il cor___ fe_del.

E voi pian_te, e fior sin_ce_ri, che o_ra in af_fia il pianto ama_ro, di_te a lui, che amor___ più ra_ro mai ve_deste___ sot_to al ciel, sotto al ciel.___ Zef_fi_retti lu_sin_ghieri, deh vo_la_

del,   che mi serbi il cor ___ fe _ del,_____ il

cor ___ fe _ del,_____ il cor ___ fe _ del.

[6] D'ORESTE, D'AJACE

Allegro assai

ferro il do_lo_re in me fi_ni_rà; o un ferro il do_lo_re, in me fi_ni_

rà,_____ in me___ fi_ni

ra,_____ in me___ fi_ni_

rà. D'O.

re _ ste, d'A_ja_ce ho in se _ noi tor_men_ti, d'A_

Die Entführung aus dem Serail

The Abduction from the Seraglio
к384 (1782)

dass in we-nig Ta-gen so Lieb' als Treu entweicht, macht, dass in we-nig

Ta - gen so Lieb' als Treu ent-seicht, _____

_____ so Lieb' als Treu entweicht. Durch Zärtlichkeit und Schmeicheln,Gefälligkeit und

Scher-zen er - o-bert man die Her - zen der gu-ten Mädchen leicht, der.

gu - ten Mädchen leicht. Doch mür-risches Be - feh - len, und pol-tern, zanken,

pla-gen, und poltern, zan-ken, pla-gen, macht, dass in we-nig Ta-gen so

Lieb' als Treu ent-weicht, _ _ _ _ 30

Lieb' als Treu ent-weicht. _ _ _ _ Durch

Zärtlichkeit und Schmeicheln, Ge-fälligkeit und Scherzen er o-bert man die

Her-zen der gu-ten Mädchen leicht.

[9] WELCHER WECHSEL HERRSCHT IN MEINER SEELE —TRAURIGKEIT

Adagio.

Recitative

Welcher Wechsel

herrscht in meiner seele, seit dem Tag, da uns das Schicksal trennte!

O Belmont! hin sind die Freu-den, die ich sonst an dei-ner Sei - te

wurmzer nag-ten Ro - se, gleich dem Gras im Win-ter-moo-se, welkt mein ban-ges

Le - ben hin, mein ban - ges Le - ben hin. Selbst der

Luft darf ich nicht sa-gen mei - ner See-le bit-tern Schmerz

mei - ner See - le bit - tern Schmerz; denn un-wil-lig ihn zu

Schmerz, mei-ner, See-le bit-tern Schmerz: dem un-willig ihn zu tra-gen, haucht sie al-le mei-ne Kla — — — — gen wieder in mein armes Herz, wie-der in mein ar — mes Herz, wieder in mein ar — mes Herz, wieder in mein ar — — — mes, ar-mes Herz.

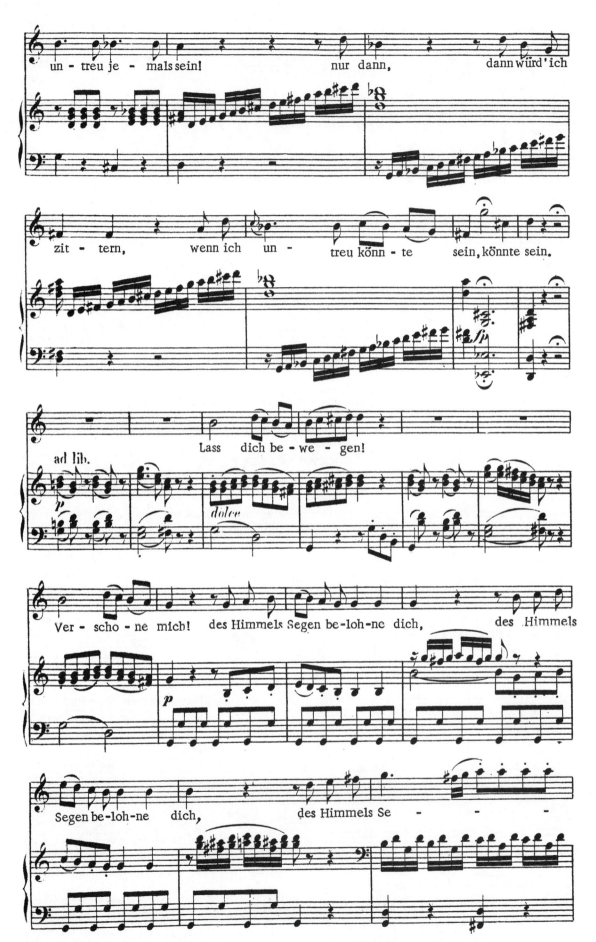

*optional cut to * on p. 69, fourth system

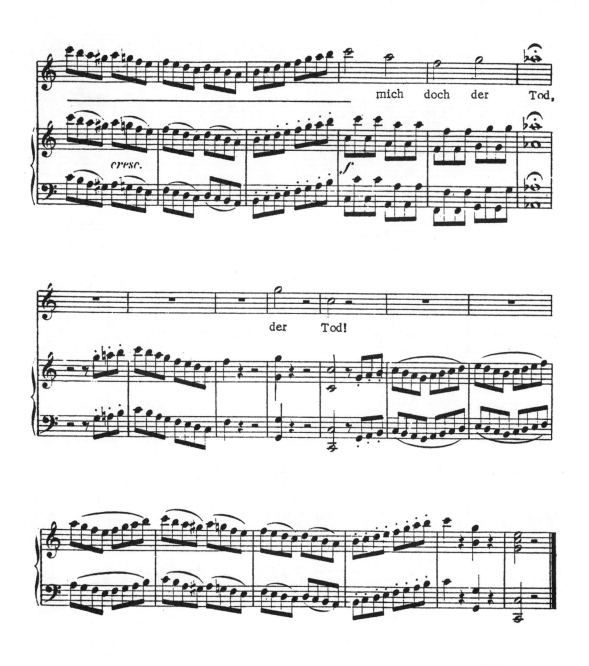

mich doch der Tod,

der Tod!

Freud' und Ju-bel pro-phe-zeih'n, Freud' und Ju-bel pro-phe - zeih'n, pro-phe-

zeih'n. Welche Won-ne, wel-che Lust herrscht nun-mehr in mei-ner Brust, wel - che

Won-ne, welche Lust herrscht nunmehr in meiner Brust! Ohne

Aufschub will ich sprin-gen, und ihr gleich die Nachricht

bringen, und mit La-chen, und mit Scherzen ihrem schwachen, fei - gen

Le Nozze di Figaro

The Marriage of Figaro
K492 (1786)

[12] NON SÒ PIÙ COSA SON, COSA FACCIO

Non sò più cosa son, cosa faccio: or di foco, ora sono di ghiaccio, o _ gni donna cangiar di co _ lo _ re, o _ gni donna mi fa palpi _ tar, o _ gni donna mi fa pal _ pi _ tar, o _ gni don _ na mi fa pal pi _ tar. So _ lo ai nomi d'amor, di di _ letto mi si

ALLᵒ VIVACE.

tur_ba, mi s'al_tera il pet_to, e a par_la_re mi sforza d'a_

_mo_re un de_si_o, un de_sio ch'io non

pos_so spie_gar, un de_si_o, un de_sio ch'io non

posso spie_gar..................... Non so più co_sa son, cosa faccio: or di

foco, ora so_no di ghiaccio, ogni donna cangiar di co_lo_re, ogni don_na mi fa palpi_

sè: par_lo d'amor ve_glian_do, par_lo d'amor so_gnan_do,

a l'acqua, a l'om_bra, ai monti, ai fio_ri, a l'erbe, ai fon_ti, a

l'e_co, a l'a_ria, ai ven_ti, che il suon de' vani ac_cen_ti por_tano via con sè....,

Adagio.

por_ta_no via con sè...... E se non ho chi m'oda, e se non ho chi

Adagio.

I.ᵐᵒ Tempo.

m'oda, par_lo d'amor con me, con me........ par_lo d'amor con me.

[13] PORGI, AMOR

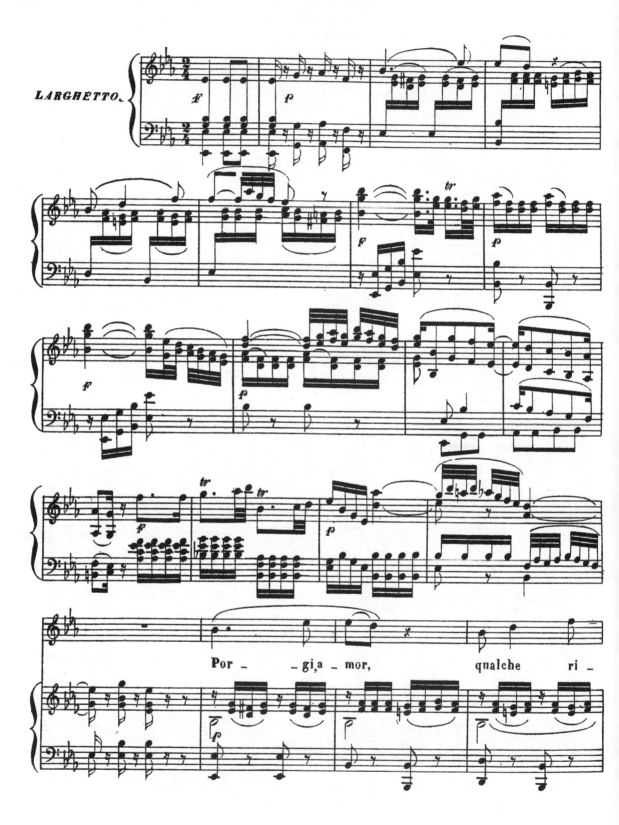

Por — gi, a — mor,   qualche   ri —

s'io l'ho nel cor. Quel _ lo ch'io pro _ vo vi........ri _ di _
_ rò, è per me nuo _ vo, ca _ pir nol so.
Sen _ to un af _ fet _ to pien di de _ sir, ch'o _ ra è di _
_ let _ to, ch'o _ ra è mar _ tir; ge _ lo, e poi sen _ to

l'al _ ma avvam _ par, e in un mo _ men _ to tor _ no a ge_

_lar. Ri _ cerco un be _ ne fuo _ ri di me:

non so chi il tie _ ne, non so co _ s'è; sospiro e ge_mo senza vo_

_ler. palpito e tre_mo senza sa_per; non trovo pa_ce not_te nè di, ma pur mi

[15] **VENITE, INGINOCCHIATEVI!**

La faccia o_ra vol_ge_temi.

O _ là! quegli occhi a me, o _ là! quegli oc_chi a me, drit_

_tissimo, drit_tissimo: guar _ da_temi, guar _ da_temi.

cres:

f p

Ma _ dama qui non è.   La faccia ora vol _ getemi:

o_la, quegli occhi a me, drit_tissimo: guarda_temi. Ma_

_da _ ma, Ma _ dama qui non è, Ma _ da _ ma qui non è.

Restate fermo, or via gi_ratevi: guar

_datemi! bravo! Più

Recitative

E Su_san_na non vien? sono ansio_sa di sa_

_per come il Con_te ac_col_se la proposta. Alquanto ardi_to il pro_

_getto mi par! e ad u_no sposo sì vi_va_ce e ge_lo_so!...

Ma che mal c'è? cangiando i miei ve_

_sti_ti con quel_li di Su_san_na, ei suoi co' mie_i...

al favor del_la not_te... Oh cie_lo! a qual u_mil sta_to fa_ta_le

io son ri_dot_ta da un con_sor_te cru_del, che do_po a_

_ver_mi con un misto i_nau_di_to d'in_fe_del_tà, di ge_lo_si_a, di

sdegni, prima a _ ma_ta, in_di of_fe_sa e al_fin tra_

_di_ta, fammi or cercar da u_na mia serva a_i_ta!

Aria

Do _ ve so _ no i bei mo _ men _ ti di dol _ cez _ za e

ANDANTE.

di pia _ cer.......? do _ ve an _ da _ ro i giu _ ra _ men _ ti

di quel labbro menzo _ gner, di quel lab _ bro men _ zo _ gner?

Perchè mai, se in pian _ ti e in pene per me

Ah! se al_men la mia co_stan_za nel lan_gui_re aman _do o _gnor mi por_

ALLEGRO.

_tas_se u _na spe_ran_za di can_giar l'ingra_to cor, di can_giar........ l'in_

_gra _ to cor!

ah!   se al _ men la mia co _ stan_za,

ah,   se al _ men la mia co _ stan _ za nel lan _

_ gui _ re a _ man _ do o _ gnor.....mi por _ tas _ se u _ na spe _ ran _ za di can _

_ giar l'in _ gra _ to   cor! mi por _ tas _ se   u _ na speran _ za   di can _

_ giar.................................... l'ingra _ to   cor, di can _ giar.....................

[17] L'HO PERDUTA! ME MESCHINA!

ANDANTE.

L'ho per_du_ta! me me_schi_na! ah chi sa do_ve sa_rà? ah chi sa do_ve sa_rà? non la tro_vo, non la tro_vo, l'ho per_

ALL⁰ VIVACE ASSAI.

Recitative

Giunse alfin il momento che go_drò senza af_fanno in braccio al_l'i_dol mi_o.

Ti_mide cu_re! u_sci_te dal mio pet_to, a tur_bar non ve_ni_te il mio di_

_letto! Oh come par che all'amo_roso

foco l'ameni_tà del lo_co, la terra e il ciel ri_sponda!

Come la notte i furti miei seconda!

ANDANTINO.

Aria

Deh vie_ni, non tar_dar, o gio_ia bel_la! vieni ove amo_re per goder t'ap_pel_la, fin_

_chè non splenda in ciel nottur_na fa_ce, fin_chè l'aria è ancor bruna e il mon_do

ta_ce. Qui mor_mora il ru_

_scel, qui scher_za l'au_ra, che col dolce su_surro il cor ri_stau_ra; qui

ri_dono i fio_ret_ti e l'er_ba è fre_sca, ai piace_ri d'amor qui tut_to a_

_de_sca. Vie _ ni, ben mi _ o, tra que_ste pian_te a _ sco _ se!

vie _ _ _ ni, vie_ni! ti vo'la fron_te in_co_ro_nar.............

........di ro _ se, ti vo' la fron _ te in_co_ro_nar...........................

.......inco_ro_nar........ di ro _ se.

Don Giovanni

к527 (1787)

[19] A<small>H</small>! <small>FUGGI IL TRADITOR</small>!

cre - der a quel cor; e na - sca il tuo ti - mor dal mio

— pe-ri - glio, ah fug - gi, fug - gi! ah

fug - gi il tra-di - tor! non lo la-sciar più dir; il

labbro è men - ti - tor, fal-la - ce il ci - glio, il

lab - bro è men - ti - tor, fal - la - - - ce il ci - glio, sì, fal - la - - - - ce il ci - glio!

[20] OR SAI CHI L'ONORE

chie-de il tuo cor! Ram - men-ta la pia-ga, ri -

mi - ra di san-gue! Ven-det - ta ti ___ chieg - go, la

chie-de il tuo ___ cor, ___ la ___

chie-de il tuo cor, ven-det - ta ti chieg - go, la chie-de il tuo

[21] Batti, batti

Andante grazioso.

Bat - ti, bat-ti, o bel Ma - set - to, la tua po - ve - ra Zer-

li - na: sta - rò qui come a - gnel - li - na le tue bot-te ad a - spet-

tar. Bat - ti, bat-ti la tua Zer - li - na; sta - rò

qui, sta-rò qui le tue botte ad a - spet - tar.

Lascie-rò straziar mi il cri - ne,

Lascie-rò cavar-mi gli occhi, e_ le ca-re tue ma-
ni-ne lie-ta poi sa-prò ba-ciar, sa-prò___ ba-
ciar, ba-ciar, sa-prò,___ sa-prò ba-
ciar.
hand.
Bat-ti,_ batti,o_ bel Ma-
set-to, la_ tua po-ve-ra Zer-li-na! sta-rò qui come a-gnel-

li - na le tue botte ad a - spet-tar. O bel Ma-sét-to!

Bat - ti, bat-ti! sta-rò qui, sta-rò qui le tue botte ad a - spet-

tar. Ah, lo ve - do,

non hai co - re, ah non hai

co - re, ah, lo ve - do, non hai co - re. Pa-ce, pa-ce o vi - ta

Allegro.

[22] VEDRAI, CARINO

Grazioso.

Ve - drai, ca - ri - no, se sei buo - ni - no, che bel ri - me-di-o ti vo-glio dar! ___ E na-tu - ra - le, non dà di - sgu - sto, e lo spe - zia - le non lo sa far, no, non lo sa far, no, non lo sa far. ___ E un cer - to bal-sa-mo

che por-to ad-dos - so, da-re t'el pos - so, se il vuoi pro - var.

Sa - per vor - re - sti

do - ve mi sta, do - ve, do - ve, do-ve mi sta?

Sen - ti - lo bat - te - re,

Toc - ca mi quà, sen - ti - lo

bat - te - re, sen ti - lo bat - te - re,   toc - ca-mi

A-per-to veg-gio il ba-ra-tro mortal!

Mi - se-raElvi-ra! che con-tra-sto d'af-fet-ti,

in sen ti nasce!

Per-chè que-sti so-spi-ri?

e quest' am-ba-scie?

Aria

Mi tra-dì_quell' al-ma in-gra-ta, quell' al - ma in - gra-ta, in - fe - li - ce, o

lui, per lui pie - tà. Mi trá - di quell'al-ma in-gra-ta, quell'

al - ma in-gra-ta, in - fe - li - ce, o Di - o! mi fa, in - fe - li - ce o

Di - o! mi fa, in - fe - li - ce o Di-o! o Dio! mi fa!

Quan-do sen-to il mio tor - men-to, il mio tor-men-to, di ven-det - ta il

cor fa - vel-la, ma se guar-do il suo ci - men - to,

[24] CRUDELE?—TROPPO MI SPIACE—NON MI DIR

Recitative ... Larghetto.

Cru-de-le? Ah no, mio be-ne!

Risoluto.

Troppo mi spia-ce al-lon-ta-nar-ti un ben che lun-ga-men-te la nostr' al-ma de-si-a.

Ma il mondo, oh Di-o! non se-

dur la co-stan-za del sen-si-bil mio core; ab-ba-stan-za per te mi parla a-

no - sci la mia fè. Cal - ma,

calma il tuo tor - mento, Se di duòl non vuoi ch'io

mo - ra, se di duol non vuoi ch'io mo - ra, non vuoi ch'io mo - ra.

cresc. f

Non mi dir, bell' i- -dol mi - o, che son

p

i - o cru - del __ con te;   cal - ma, cal - ma   il tuo tor -

men - to,   se di duol __   non vuoi   ch'io

mo - ra,   non   vuoi ch'io mo - _ - ra!

Allegretto moderato.

For - se, forse un giorno il __ cie - lo __ an -

co - ra sen - ti - rà,__ sen-ti - rà pie - tà__ di me! __ forse un

giorno il cielo an-co-ra sen-ti - rà _____

pie - tà _____ di me, sen - ti-rà pie -

tà, _____ pie - tà di me, sen - ti -

Così fan tutte

к588 (1790)

Recitative

Ah sco_sta_ti, pa_ven_ta il tri_sto ef_fet_to d'un di_spe_ra_to af_fet_to!

All.º assai

Chiu_di quel_le fi_ne_stre...

o_dio la lu_ce... odio l'aria che spiro...

o_dio me stessa...

Chi scherni_sce il mio duol, chi__ mi con_so_la?

ne_sto, da_rò al_l'Eu_me_ni_di

se vi_va re_sto col suo_no or_

_ri_ _bi_le de'

miei so_ _spir, de' mie_i so_

_spir, de' mie_i so_ _spir.

Sma nie im pla _ca bi _ li_____ che m'a _ gi _ ta _ te, den _ tro que_st'a _ ni_ma_____ più non ces _ _sa _ te, fin _ ché l'an _ go _ scia mi fa mo _ rir, mi _ fa mo _

se vi _ va re _ sto,

col suo _ no or _ ri _ bi _ le, col suo _ no or _ ri _ bi _

_ le de' miei_____ so _

_ spir,____ de'____ mie _ i so _ _ spir,____ de'____

mie _ i so _ _ spir.

[26] In uomini, in soldati

fa_te sen_tir, per ca_ri_tà, non vi fa_te sen_tir, per ca_ri_

_tà!

Allegretto

Di pasta si_mile son tutti quan_ti, son tutti

quan_ti: le fronde mo_bi_li, l'aure inco_stan_ti han più de_gli uomi_ni sta_bi_li_

_tà. Men_ti_te la_grime, fal_laci sguar_di,

voci ingan_ne_voli, vez_zi bu_giar_di, son le pri_ma_rie

lor qua _ li _ tà, son le pri _ ma _ rie _____ lor qua _ li _ tà. In noi non

a _ mano che il lor di _ let _ to, poi ci di _ spre _ giano, ne _ gan ci af_

_fet _ to, né val da' bar _ bari chieder pie_tà, né val da' bar _ bari chieder pie_

_tà, chie _ der pie _ tà, chie_der pie_tà.

Paghiam,o fem_mi_ne, d'ugual mo_ne_ta questa ma_le_fi_ca razza in di_

_scre_ta; amiamper co_modo, per va_ni_tà, amiamper co_modo, per va_ni_

_tà, amiamper co_modo, per va_ni_tà, la ra la,

la ra la, la ra la la, amiamper co_modo, per va_ni_tà,

amiamper co_mo_do, per va_ni_tà, la ra la,
la_ra la, la_ra la la, amiamper co_modo, per va_ni_tà,___ amiamper
co_modo, per va_ni_tà,___ amiamper co_modo, per vani_tà.

[27] TEMERARI, SORTITE—COME SCOGLIO —RISPETTATE, ANIME INGRATE

Recitative

Te_me_ra_ri, sorti_te; fuori da questo lo_co: e non pro_fa_ni l'a_li_to in_fau_sto degl'in_fa_mi det_ti nostro cor, nostro o_recchio, e nostri af_fet_ti! In_van per voi, per gli altri in_van si cerca le no_stre alme sedur, l'in_tat_ta fe_de che per noi già si die_de ai ca_ria_

_manti   sapremlo_ro ser_bar   in _ fi_no a morte,

a dispetto del mondo   e del_la sorte.

Aria

Andante maestoso   Co _ me scoglio   im_

_mo _ to re_sta   con _ tra i ven_ti   e

so_la,   e po_trà la mor_te

so_la, la mor _ _ te_ so_la far che

can _ gi af _ fet _ to il cor,   far che

can _ gi, far che can _ gi af _ fet _ to il

cor, far che can _ gi af _ fet _ _ _ _ _

UNA DONNA A QUINDICI ANNI
—DEE IN UN MOMENTO

_tar___ i_bei per_chè,___ fin_ger ri _ so, fin_ger pian _ ti, in_ven_

_tar___ i_be _ i per _ chè.

Dee in un mo_

Allegretto

_p_

_men _ to dar retta a cen _ to, con le pu_pil _ le par_lar con mil _ le,

dar spe_me a tut _ ti sian bel_li o brut _ ti, sa_per na_

_tri _ na; vi _ va De _ spi _ na che sa ser _ vir, ____ che sa ser _ vir.)

Dee in un mo _ men _ to dar ret _ ta a cen _ to, col le pu _ pil _ le par _ lar con

mil _ le,

dar spe _ me a tut _ ti, sian bel _ li, o

brut _ ti, sa _ per na _ scon _ der _ si senza con _ fon _ dersi, senza arros _ si _ re saper men _

vo _ glio far _ si ub _ bi _ dir, sì, far _ si ub _ bi _

_ dir, _ sì, _ far _ si ub _ bi _ dir. (Par ch'abbian

gu _ sto di tal dot _ tri _ na; vi _ va De _ spi _ na che sa ser _ vir, vi _ va De _

_ spi _ na che sa ser _ vir, vi _ va De _ spi _ na che sa ser _ vir, _ che sa ser _ vir, _ che sa ser _ vir.)

[29] PER PIETÀ, BEN MIO, PERDONA
—A CHI MAI MANCÒ

Rondò

voglia l'ardir mio, la mia ___ co-stanza, per - derà ___

la ri _ membranza, che vergogna e or _ ror ___ mi fa,

che vergogna, che ver _ go _ _ _ gna e orror ___ mi ___

fa. Per _ pie _ tà, _ ben mio, per _ do _ na al _ l'er_

fe _ de que _ sto _ va _ no, in gra _ to cor, si do _ ve _ a mi _ glior mer _

_ ce _ de, _ ca _ ro be _ ne, al tuo can _ dor, ca _ ro _

cresc. *f*

be _ _ _ _ ne al tuo can _

p

_ dor. Per pie _ tà, ben mio, per _

dolce

_do_ _na_ al _ l'er _ ror d'u _ n'al _ ma a _ _man_ _te;_ svene_rà quest'em_pia vo_glia l'ardir mio, la mia co_ _stan_ _za,_ perde_rà_ la_ ri_mem_bran_za, che ver_ _gogna e orror mi_ fa. A_ chi_ mai mancò di fe_de que_sto

va _ no, ingra _ to cor, si do _ ve _ a mi glior mer _ ce _ de, ca _ ro

be _ ne, al tuo can _ dor, ca _ ro_ be _

_ ne, al_ tuo can _

_ dor, a chi mai man _

cò_____ di_____ fe_de que_sto va_no, in_ -gra_ to_ cor,_____ que_ sto va_no, que_ sto va_ -no, ingra_ to_____ cor, si do_ -vea_____ miglior mer_ce_de, ca_ro be_ne, al tuo_ can_

-dor,   ca - ro___ be - ne,   al tuo_____ can -

-dor,___   ca - ro be - ne,   ca - ro

be___ - ne,al tuo   can - dor,   ca - ro___ be - ne,al tuo can -

-dor,   ca - ro___ be - ne,al tuo can - dor,___   ca - ro be - ne,___caro

t'em _ pie di di _ sgu _ sto se ten _ ti di pu _ gnar;

porta dol _ cez _ za e gu _ sto se tu lo la _ sci far, ma

t'em _ pie di ___ di _ sgu _ sto se ten _ ti di ___ pu _ gnar.

___ E a _ mo _ re un la _ dron _ cel _ lo, un ser _ pen tel _ lo è a-

_mor, ___ ei to _ glie e dà _ la pa _ ce, la pa _ ce

come gli pia _ ce ai cor. Se nel tuo pet _ to ei sie _ de, s'egli ti bec _ ca

qui, fa tut _ to quel ch'ei chie _ de _ che anch'io fa _ rò _ co _ sì; _

se nel tuo pet _ to ei sie _ de, s'egli ti bec _ ca

qui, qui, qui, qui, fa tut _ to quel ch'ei chie _ de _ che an

_ ch'io fa _ rò _ co _ sì, s'egli ti bec _ ca, s'e _ gli ti bec _ ca, s'e _ gli ti

becca, ti becca, ti becca, ti becca, ti bec _ _ _ ca, fa tut _ to quel _ ch'ei chie _ de, ch'ei chie _ de che an_ _ch'io fa _ rò co _ sì, co _ sì, che anch'io fa _ rò co _ sì, co _ sì, che an_ _ch'io fa _ rò co _ sì.

Die Zauberflöte

The Magic Flute
к620 (1791)

[31] O zitt're nicht, mein lieber Sohn!
—Zum Leiden bin ich auserkoren

Streben! Ich musste sie mir rauben se - hen. „Ach helf't! ach helf't!" war Alles,was sie
fe - se ancormi so - nd-no d'intorno al cor.___ Oh ciel! oh ciel! la mi-se-ra gri-

sprach; al-lein ver - - ge-benswar ihr Flehen, denn meine Hül - fe war zu schwach,
dò. A - di - fen-der-ti, Pa - mi-na, ahi! la ma - dre non ba - stò,

Allegro moderato.

denn meine Hülfe, mei-ne Hül-fe war___ zu schwach.
ahi! la ma - dre, la ma-dre non___ ba - stò.

Du, du, du wirst sie zu be-frei-en ge - hen,
Va! ri - tor - - la,ri-tor-la al ra-pi - to - ro,

Allegro assai.

Der Höl_le Ra _ che kocht in mei_nem Her_zen;
Gli angui d'in-fer _ no sen-to-mi nel pet-to;

Tod und Ver_zweiflung, Tod und Ver-zweif-lung flam _
Me _ gae-_ra, A-let-to son d'in-_ tor-no a me,_

_ met um mich her! Fühlt nicht durch dich Sa_ra_stro To_des_
_ d'in-tor-no a me! Svel-_ ga al fel-lon, svel-ga Pa-mi-na il

schmerzen, Sa_ra_stro To_des_schmer_zen, so bist du mei_ne
co _ re, svelga Pa-mi-na il co _ re! Seil reo non muo-re,

Toch_ter nim_mer mehr, so bist du mein', meine Toch_ter nim_mer
fi_glia mia non è, se il reo non muor, figlia mia non

al - le Ban-de der Na - tur, wenn nicht durch dich Sa - ra-stro wird er-
ser cru- -del, es - ser cru - del. Svel - ga al fel - lon, Pa - mi - na, svelga il

blas - - - sen! Hört, hört, hört,
co - - - re! Ciel! ciel! l'or ren - - - -

Rache-götter, hört der Mutter Schwur!
do mio vo-to, ah! as-colta, o ciel!

La Clemenza di Tito

к621 (1791)

Schlägt mir dein Herz voll Lie - be, lass Furcht und Argwohn schwinden!
Deh, se pia - cer mi vuo - i, la - scia i so - spet - ti tuo - i,

Du kannst sie ü - ber - winden, sie ü - ber - winden, mein Wort, ___ mein
ah nò, non mi stan - car, nò, non mi stan - car, nò, con que - - sto mo -

Wort zum Un - - ter - pfand! Du kannst sie ü - ber -
le - sto du - - bi - tar, non mi stan - car con

win - den, mein Wort ___ zum Un - ter - pfand!
que - sto mo - le - - - sto du - bi - tar,

Lass Furcht und Argwohn schwinden, du kannst sie ü - ber - win - den, mein
non mi stan - car con que - sto, non mi stan - car con que - sto mo -

Wo Wort und Treu - e thro-nen, reicht
Chi sem - pre in gan - ni a-spet - ta, al -

Lie - be dir die Hand, reicht Lie-be, reicht Lie-be, reicht
let - ta ad in - gan - nar, al - - let - ta, al - - let - ta, al -

Lie-be, ja, reicht Lie-be dir die Hand! Schlägt mir dein
let - ta,al - let-ta,al - - let - ta ad in - gan - nar. Deh se pia -

Herz, dein Herz voll Lie - be, lass Furcht und
cer, pia - cer mi vuo - i; la - - scia i so-

Arg-wohn, lass Furcht und Arg - - wohn schwinden!
spet - ti, la - scia i so-spet - - ti tuo - i.

[35] S'ALTRO CHE LAGRIME

Tempo di Menuetto.

Thrä-nen der Zärtlichkeit um den Ge-
Sal - tro che la-cri-me per lui non

lieb-ten sind nicht das Mit-tel, das ihn be-freit,
ten - ti tutto il tuo piange-re non gio-ve - rà,

sind nicht das Mit-tel, das ihn be-freit, das ihn be-
tutto il tuo piangere non gio-ve - rà, non gio - ve -

freit. Des Mit-leids tie-fenSchmerz zeigt ihm durch Tha-ten,
rà. A quest' in - u - ti - le pie - tà che sen-ti,

sonstgleicht das Mit-leid der Grau-sam-keit, der Grau-sam-
oh quan-to è si-mi-le la cru-del-tà, la cru-del-

Allegro   *Recitative*

Ec_co il punto,   o   Vi_

tel_lia, d'e_sa_mi_nar la tua co_stanza.   A_vrai va_lor, che

ba_sti   a ri_mi_rar e _ sangue   il tuo Se_sto fe_del?

Se_sto che t'a_ma   più del_la vi_ta su_a? che per tua

col_pa di_ven_ne re_o?   che t'ub_bi_dì, cru_de_le? che ingiu_sta t'a_do_

rò? che in faccia a mor_te si gran fe_de ti ser_ba? e tu frat_

tan_to, non i_gno_ta a te stes_sa, an_drai tran_quil_la al

ta_la_mo d'Augusto? Ah! mi ve_dre _ _ _ i sem_pre Se_sto d'in_

tor_no. E l'au_re e i sas_si te_me_rei che lo_qua_ci

mi sco_pris_se_ro a Tito.

A pie di suoi va_dasi il tut_to a pa _ le _ sar. Si sce_mi

il de _lit_to di Se_sto, se scu_sar non si può, col fal _ lo mi_o. D'im

pe_ri e d'i_me_ne_i spe _ ran_ze, ad_di_o.

Larghetto

Rondò

Non più di fio _ ri va_ghe ca _ te _ ne discenda I_

me _ ne ad in _ trec _ ciar. Stret _ ta fra bar _ ba _ re a _ spre ri _

tor _ te veg _ go la mor _ te ver me avanzar, veg _ go la

mor _ _ _ te _ ver me a _ van _ zar. Non più di fio _ _ ri

va _ ghe ca _ te _ ne di _ scen _ da I _ me _ ne ad in _ trec _

car,   non più di fio _ ri   va _ ghe   ca_

Allegro

te _ ne   di _ scenda I _ me _ ne   ad in _ trec _ ciar.

In _ _ fe _ li _ ce!   qual'   or _ ro _ re!

Ah!_____ di me   che si   di _ rà,   che si di_

rà?   Chi ve _ des_se il mio do_

lo _ re, pur a _ vria di me pie _ tà,   chi ve _ desse

il mio do _ lo _ re,   pur a _ vria di me pie _

tà,   pur a _ vria di me pie _

tà.

Non più di fio _ ri va _ ghe ca _ te _ ne   di _ scen _ da I _

me _ ne ad in_trec_ciar. Stret _ ta fra bar_ba_re

a _ spre ri_tor_te, veg_go la mor_te

ver me a_van_zar, veg _ go la mor_te

ver me a _ van_zar! In _ fe_

li _ ce! qual' or_ro_re! ah di me che

des _ se il mio do _ lo _ re, pur a _ vria di me pie _ tà,

in _ fe li _ ce! qual'___ or _ ro _ re! Non più di fio _ ri va ghe ca _

te _ ne di scenda I _ me _ ne ad in _ trec _ ciar. Stret _ ta fra bar _ ba _ re a spreri _

tor _ te, veg go la mor _ te ver me a _ van _ zar.

Chi ve _ des _ se il mio do _ lo _ re, pur a _ vria di me pie _

tà. chi ve_des_se il mio do_lo _ re, pur a_vria di me pie_tà, _____ pie_tà. ___ di me pie _ tà, _____ pie_ tà, ___ di me pie _ tà, di me, di me ___ pie _ tà, pur a _ vria di me pie_

Andante maestoso